Reflections of Humanity

(A tapestry of perceptions)

Reflections of Humanity

(A tapestry of perceptions)

GARY LaCARRUBBA

ARPress
ILLUMINATING IDEAS
EMPOWERING VOICES

ARPress LLC
45 Dan Road Suite 5
Canton MA 02021
Hotline: 1(888) 821-0229
Fax: 1(508) 545-7580

Ordering Information:
Quantity sales. Special discounts are available on quantity purchases by corporations, associations, and others. For details, contact the publisher at the address above.

Printed in the United States of America.

ISBN-13: Softcover   979-8-89330-864-8
          eBook   979-8-89330-865-5

Library of Congress Control Number: 2024902589

To all those who would not let me lose sight of the dreams, in spite of myself.

Reflections of Humanity
(a tapestry of perceptions)
Table of Contents

A note to the reader:

This work has been described as a collection of introspective pieces that range from the classic yet never overdone themes to a few that could be wrestled with regarding interpretation and meaning. Two of the favorite things noted were the content/theme and voice of the work. While the topics are sometimes heavy and complicated the tone and voice used to present the subject matter follow a lighter, almost Silverstein-esque pattern with the light tone carrying the heavy message quite well. The narrative style chosen in the piece titled "Evolution" essentially condenses the Bible onto a few pages of stanzas. It's impressive that this was done without having to resort to an epic the likes of "Paradise Lost."

The parallel between the unfolding of the Biblical story with the *evolution* of human nature as well as posing the question of where humanity moves from the present was also thought provoking and enjoyable. Some of these works were simple, but in the sense that the simplicity lacked pretense. In many cases, these works approached the educated vs. intelligence vs. wise reflection well, which contributed to the overall enjoyment of reading this collection.

The Paradox

Totally absurd---yet, completely undisputed
Contradiction of terms; not to be doubted
Both ends of the spectrum represented
Not to mention, in between those ends
Lord! How complex; this thing called a paradox

What it boils down to
Quite simply; it's true
One can be right, while another is too
Neither may agree with you
Which only means; you can be right too

The world is an awfully big place
Yet, much to small for such a silly race
One man's floor---another's ceiling
Can't they see? It's just a part of living

One tries to prove another wrong
Only to make their own position strong
Yet, as their opinion they speak
They may watch the other grow weak

Now they've hurt someone
To prove a point; only to espouse an opinion
This in the guise of being just
Rather than simply accepting the paradox

Evolution

(a view of Creationism)

In the beginning, there was space and time only
And over time, there formed energy
God's own breath the everlasting key
And through this energy; there formed particles
And through the formation of these ions; there came a cloud
And as this cloud polarized; there formed another cloud
And like scales; they balanced each other
And the energy displaced a greater area

Gradually; this displacement did increase
The clouds moving farther apart; north to south---west to east
Moving as an ebbing tide amidst night's dark
Farther and Farther apart; now beginning to form an arc
Spinning slowly end over end; growing more dense
Then; as the laws of nature did commence
Each move closer to the other from opposite ends
The displaced energy causing them to hurl
Like stones from a sling; they did sail

Gaining in speed and mass
Unavoidably on a collision course
And as like found like amidst the ensuing fallout
There began our universe; and the planets came about
Hastily spinning; each into its own orbit
Friction giving way to light; bright, burning light, when done
And this light was to be called the Sun
Heat and cold working hand and hand
And they begot life; as it came to be known
Various forms; all sizes and shapes

And these things did happen over ages
Plants and trees covered the land
Fish in the waters; above the sand
Birds in the sky; having been destined to fly
Insects and animals to belie
And then; God's ultimate creation
There came that which was to be known as human
Formed in Mother Nature's own womb

Began as a simple chemical process
Constantly growing and changing---Oh! So complex
Literally born of the dust and ashes of those cloud formations
Intelligent energy: One to be man, one to be woman
All the ability to work, play and please
Then; a more fateful day; innocence would cease
Knowledge of jealousy; fruit of the forbidden tree
Man beat woman; turned love to hate and wanton need
Punished for her own naivete; maybe for her greed

How senseless that man truly was

Brutalizing such holy innocence; God's original dove

Cast out of paradise; that home of unconditional love

Now to begin a more perilous journey over eons to come

Woman having been with child when beaten

Sowed hatred unknowingly within her womb

Then came her firstborn; a constant reminder to that brutal one

Her immorality's sole representation

Or so he believed out of hand

Too proud, too stupid, to ever consider

The immorality belonged to him; not her

He, who made her so afraid

Only to make her his lifelong slave

Perpetuating the error by mistreating wife and child

Unable to see his own guilt; his own guile

From one generation to the next; this legacy did stray

Gender being lost along the way

Made no difference who would pay

Spouse against spouse

Parent against offspring

Sibling against sibling

One's will against the other's meaning

Seldom a truly cooperative effort

As it was intended; from the outset

Mankind had become its own worst enemy

No end was to be found to this adversity

And that was very clear for all to see

Weakness was the prevailing factor in their souls
Man blaming God for his woes
Unable or unwilling to accuse himself
Claiming he was naked because of his shame
Disparaging anyone other than self to hide that shame
Condemned self and child with that blame
Attempting to elude responsibility
What a fool's errand was created
As their own foibles they evaded

Thousands of years passed without any real change
Then; one was conceived immaculately
A true child of God, Most High---Our Creator
No doubt mankind's redemption
Demonstrated love for life and the living; without exception
Teaching the Sciences and Philosophy; among other matters of destiny
Showing the true path of our evolution
Condemned to death for his perfection
How dare he strip his ancestors of their beloved deception

What nerve; claiming they had any responsibility
God among humans---that couldn't be
Kill him! They shouted and screamed
The devil's very own---rid us of this vermin
And kill him they did; this one born to redeem
Before he dies though; his purpose he did achieve
Planted a seed within which to believe

Life was for living; couldn't have been put more simply
The cycle was now destined to break; finally

Years passed into decades
Decades to become centuries; even millennium
Yet, from one hour to the next, that seed kept growing
A different lamp had been lit within each one's sight
More and more; humanity craved that new light
How truly unique each one did feel
Breaking from that error of heritage which seemed perpetual
The Messiah had indeed come
Just as the faithful had promised; God's will had been done

How perfect---the son of God was the son of man too
Planted a seed called faith; seemingly absurd
Provided the tools with which to cultivate; our words
Gave instruction for cultivation; Perseverance to be that sword
Taught how to live a life for the living; compassion was His claim
Combined his talents and it became true wisdom
Wisdom; a fertile place for faith to flourish
Each soul sowing and reaping their own fruits and rewards
Some good---some bad; Some pursuing hope---some wishing they had

Can anyone be completely perfect
Not even that one; submitted to his own death
Teaching faith of a mustard seed; pure thought
Yet, when asked to defend; wouldn't talk
His very silence led to his demise

Yet, had he spoken freely---himself he would despise
Didn't have the heart to defend his being
Thorns of anguish clouding his meaning
Stripped of his garments as well as his dignity

Removed from his cross upon his death
To be placed in a tomb for his final test
Soon thereafter to arise
Instilling belief without compromise
How could he have done better
There are those who believe he did his very best
This; in the truest interest of justice
Sacrificing self so the scales would balance
Sacrificing self for the greedy---how abhorrent

Dying at the hands of his accusers
Taking to his grave the knowledge that they were the losers
Setting a precedent for martyrdom
As the one and only way into God's kingdom
Thought he must choose between God and mammon
Believing no man could serve two passions
Instead of instilling the discipline of moderation
What a shame to each and every one
What a pitiful abomination

Camels could pass through the eye of a needle
Rich men could not enter heaven with ease
Mankind should never seek to master wealth--- or should they
Never to equal God---or could they

Always to be corrupt---or would they

Eternally corrupt---using force to impose will

Slaves to God---relying upon excuses instead of fortitude

Pursuing wealth---forsaking justice instead of seeking it

Yet; is that really what was taught

Can't one pursue wealth...while seeking justice

Can't one have fortitude...without making excuses

Can't one have their way...without imposing it

Will these mountains hurl themselves into the seas

Faith is all it really takes

Faith; the ability to believe

One self's ability to master one's own needs

Be fair---by all means

Treat those in your life as kings and queens

Doing unto others; that's the rule of thumb

Watching storms pass without becoming numb

Be not another's judge in haste

No greater sin---no greater waste

Neutrality is the golden key

The lock; a concept called harmony

Not a misplaced idealism; simply a realistic altruism

Unconditional love and concern

Formulas worthy of discern

Principles to break those cold vicious cycles that seemed without end

The newest Alpha and Omega; beginning without termination

Values to consider in the love of ones fellow man
Humanity's biggest step toward becoming human
No longer babies limited to crawling
Now we are grown---now we are living
Life no longer to be a place of desolation
Living no longer to be an abomination
Herein; the true story of humanity's evolution

Peace in the world is what was intended
Peace in one's soul is what was recommended
Peace of mind to weather the storm
Peace; in every way, shape and form
Many a sculptor failing to fashion from mere flesh and bone
Once the builder's rejected stone
Now to become the cornerstone
To be humanity's most everlasting foundation
Peace alone can secure our continued evolution

End

or is it?

My Love, My World
My Life's Quest

My wealth---Your being
My Wisdom---Your compassion
My need---Your Love
My want---Your happiness
My desire---Your pleasure
My love---Your very soul

My being---The way you care for me
My compassion ---The way you inspire me
My happiness---The way you love me
My pleasure---The way you want me
My very soul---You, my love, eternally

Allowing me to be me
By knowing I love you for you
Accepting me as I am
By knowing that's how I accept you
Sating your curiosity about me
By knowing that it's who you are that enables me to be

Fulfilling me in every way

By knowing our love will always stay

Making our lives so very complete

Each of us, now having found our soulmate

Now to realize my life's quest

My Love; My World---you are the very best

Down this Path

Walking down this path called life
The way is ofttimes encumbered
Each obstacle a new challenge
Some solutions less than evident
Tenacity pushing me along the way
Meeting those perils which place me in jeopardy

Contentment is my goal
Simply yearning for peace in my soul
Free of other's lunacy
Those seeking to harm me in word and deed
Thinking to keep me as their lackey
Never once to consider my need

Gauntlets cast down each and every day
Yet; their trials never obscure my way
With a clear vision I go forth
Courage being my truest friend; the only one I brought
Fears overcome by faith never overwrought
This path; the one that I have always sought

Recalling a childhood fantasy
Living my life with no degree of certainty
Only God's will to guide me
The single thought that is my very security
Making me the target of another's jealousy
They who plot to steal my individuality

Known only to the powers that be
Their true reasons for not wanting me to be me
Why? Oh why, do they fear me so
Is it I they have come to know
Or do they see their own reflection
Causing fear to rule their soul and inspire their deception

Thus; I continue down this path
Hope; the companion of the day
My shield against all the hate
So their avarice they may not sate
My life's blood remains my own
Going down this path---Truly, I have grown

One or the Other

One thought nothing of their hostility
The other thought only to cradle me
From one; piercing hatred and aggressive disdain
From the other; a loving smile to ease the pain

Both; the recipient's of purest love
One became a shrew
The other; a dove
One; full of avarice and terror
The other; that pure loves mirror

Ones efforts, reaping little or no avail
The other's desires had to prevail
One worldly and purportedly intelligent
The other; naïve and innocent---thus, the most brilliant

One sowed seeds of hatred
The other; stood, watched and cared
One cringed as the seeds washed away
The other smiled knowingly as she got her way

One; so in a hurry to destroy
The other; so patient an ally
One to get everything she so richly deserved
The other; to get everything which she craved
One destined to fall by the wayside
The other; to take her place at my side

Can I Love

Can I love humanity
Before I accept another's individuality
Can I care for even one other person
Before I am conscious of my reason
Can I like or love each as they are
Before I take the time to care

If I cannot accomplish even these simple things
Can I expect sanity within other beings
Must not it then become my life's way
To promote the sanity that I expect in return
Or should I lose sight of my need for concern
Only to forget my innate ability to reason
Thus; I keep the will to accept that individual
Simply loving humanity with all my heart and soul

An Angel of Mercy

The one who saw what was hidden
The one who realized that it wasn't forbidden
Offering kindness in the face of despair
Without remorse, hesitation, or fear
Taking the time to understand the needs of another
As though they were mother or father, sister or brother

When fate is kind enough to bring you such a one
Pain soon departs; falling into that darkest abyss
Back from where it came; before fate's kind kiss
Such an angel could be just anyone

Easily recognized by their stature
Known by their deeds and good nature

Could this Angel of Mercy be you
Could you be the one so true
You're the only one who can answer
You're the only one who knows for sure
It's in the way you treat all others
Sharing that which alone is yours
Your gift of goodwill from yourself to another

A Folk Story

(a memory of some years ago)
Author Unknown

"What kind of place is this?"
asked a certain man.
"What kind of place are you from?"
responded the other.
"I am from a place where people tend to be mean"
was the certain man's answer.
"Well, I'm afraid that's what you can expect to find here again"
said the other.

"What kind of place is this?"
Inquired a second man.
"What kind of place are you from?"
replied the other.
"I'm from a place where people seem so indifferent"
was the second man's answer
"Well, that's pretty much the way people are here"
noted the other

"What kind of place is this?"
questioned yet a third traveler.
"What kind of place are you from?"
quried the other.
"I am from a place where people tend to be very friendly"
stated this traveler.
"Well, you'll like it here just fine, my friend"
advised the other.
"Because that's just about what you'll find here."

Reflections

(destined to provoke thought)

Who does he think he is
Oh, such arrogance with no remorse
How can that one be so despicable
So high and mighty; thinks he's so capable

What a miserable lout
Completely inflexible; no doubt
Where does he find such nerve
Constantly haranguing; such evil verve

When will he cease to be so pompous a fool
Thinks he's God's gift to the world; so cool
Why does he think himself so great
Obviously can't see the way others relate

Oh! My God!
Now I recognize that fool
I can't believe it's really so droll
That one that I hate; so evil and vain

Now, so clearly evident
I'm the one that has been so repugnant

Could this really be true
Is it really me and not you
Repeatedly, I did accuse
Only to realize, I have no excuse
Just a shoe that fits; if a hypocrite I did seduce

God knows; we can all be guilty of that
Casting aspersions at another's fault
Remaining blind to our own guilt
And all too often; perfect we are not
That being why reflections are destined to provoke thought

The Child's Birthright

Blessing or curse
Pleasure or burden's beast
Taxing Parents as they do
Testing everyone; doesn't matter who
Really just a matter of attitude
Talking to them doesn't seem to assist us
Threatening seems to do even less
Punishing is rarely productive
Beating will certainly turn them against us
Parenting---what an ordeal of interest!

Spare the rod: spoil the child
What utter nonsense is that maxim
Giving birth to centuries of abuse without concern
Is that really the basis of procreation
These that are least in size and station
One day to be the root of every nation
What legacy shall we pass on
Deserving of their adoration
Our pride and joy from the moment born
Our sons and daughters; our children

Perhaps listening is a potential solution
Hearing what they're saying from their perception
Turning their way of thinking to what is best
One never knows about a child's happiness
Sometimes; it's even they that know what's fairest
Instilling a sense of discipline is our caress
Ability to forgive; shows we can endear
A slap on the wrist may occasionally be called for
Even that; they accept with a willing spirit
When they know that it is they who truly deserve it

It is, after all, through them that our lives were blessed
Their presence here was our decision, not theirs
They did not ask to be born; to become our heirs
So why do we try so hard to suppress them
Instead of lavishing hugs and kisses upon them
That which they constantly yearn for; love and affection
Those simple rewards in which they delight
The true legacy of heritage; the child's birthright

The Truth of Wisdom

The wonder of wisdom abounds
Oft times making one's senses go round and round
One must constantly query whether coming or going
Seemingly destined to remain without ever knowing

What is this truth of wisdom
Daresay; it predates even Solomon
Enables one to perceive
Another's right to their dignity

Pointing out errors so haughtiilly
Wanting to even the score, and punish, so naughtily
Then; only to wonder weather it's worth it
As we look for a reason to forget and forgive

Let bygones be bygones; live and let live
Axioms and maxims to grow with
In the spirit of peace; for the sake of love
Reminding one of the olive branch borne by the dove

Can it be true wisdom without the truth
Just another of life's paradoxes

Thinking ourselves as clever as foxes
Then to understand what truth really is

The truth of wisdom; so sublime
Everyone makes a mistake from time to time
Only goes to show; we're all human
Not a crime; not even a sin
This thing we know as the human condition

Splendid realization; optimism's inspiration
After all is said and done
Doesn't matter whether it's beginning or end
This realization of self; that's the truth of wisdom

Who Am I

One born to soul search all life long
As a child; to improve and be grown
Then adolescence; the need to fit in
Finally; to become an adult atop that foundation
Now to place stone upon stone
As we meet each new one

The quest to search our soul still burning within
Meeting responsibility from day to day with all due concern
Crossing paths with others by varying means
Helping out when ability deems
Sometimes; no strings to consider
Others; just swapping favor for favor

Always destined to ponder and wonder
Espying the fortitude of our structure
Enhancing design and worthiness of the architecture
Who am I?
Such a nagging question
The one and only answer: I am...the first person

Evolution---Part II

(values of life with meaning)

Once upon a time…Oh! So long ago
There came a child; God's own alter ego
Conceived by yet another child of the One, Most High
As truly blessed as the heavenly bodies of the sky

Child of God; child of man
No more than a human being since his life began
Lived and died in but a few short years
His way; destined to evoke tears

Taught many things within a code called parables
Stories to unlock the laws of nature; unparalleled
Personally teaching but a handful to carry on
Each to their own task; but with a single mission

Many would believe a new religion had been born
Yet, had they understood; had they paid attention
A new religion; to be sure---a philosophical perception
Mankind does contend; thus confusing God and religion

One day to understand the sciences of that contention
Purity of heart and soul do tend
That the mind and body won't rend
Making each one's senses a finer blend

Purity of heart and soul will guarantee
Minds as well as bodies will see
What God hath joined together
Was not for men to put asunder

Just what is it this Creator did together join
This common bond; fruit of his loins
Men and woman on altars within His houses
Perhaps the flesh and spirit born to those spouses

Legend has it; in His image we're created
Pity contends that His image has been belated
Now knowing why; for ourselves, we felt sorry
Now to be free of the burden we were once forced to carry

Our ability to shun what we own
Eclipsing what we should have known
Will the day come soon
Like the sun's light reflected by the moon

We, as a race, will be that image
One created to be without blemish
Erring is human; forgiveness---divine
Erring; that part of life necessary to live and learn

Burying our dead; so life can go on again
Intellectual curiosity raising us from plane to plane
Cooperation is what we need to remain
Problem free living; no such thing---that is plain

Utopian life belongs on fantasy isle
That part of your mind beyond guile
Where pain and trauma are forbidden
As they once were in a place called Eden

Problems do have solutions
Solutions usually create new problems
Necessity again to become the mother of invention
As a certain wise man did discern

Invention? One's own faith, hope and charity
Faith enough to believe
Hope enough to relieve and achieve
Charity enough to give; as well as receive

But a few of the ethics taught
And aren't they what we've all sought
Simple as the golden rule to comprehend
Our evolution was destined
Values of life with meaning

About the Author

Gary LaCarrubba, a loving family man and avid seeker of truth, developed a profound interest in the theory of creationism and the evolution of humanity. A Roman Catholic by birth, Gary sought out the nuances learned through his faith and correlated those to various historical recordings that were available through a variety of sources that were discovered throughout his life.

During his pursuit of this endeavor, Gary became more convinced that many of the so-called mysteries of faith, although probably well intentioned in their time in most cases, appeared genuinely and purposefully misleading in what they suggested of a benevolent God. Accepting Christ as his only mentor and pursuing those teachings as they filtered down through the ages,

Gary sought to unravel those instances of curiosity left behind by that mentor. References such as "Let he who reads understand" were challenges that appeared to be provoking the reader to a deeper consciousness of the soul and the effects that our heritage places burdens on that very soul.

These works are the product of those years of fulfilling that curiosity. As a loving parent, Gary could not and would not accept that the being responsible for the creation of humanity only sought to do so to lead that creation to its demise as repeatedly suggested through the various books written on this topic throughout the annals of time.

These works are this author's perceptions of a mindset that recognizes God, Most High, as a benevolent and caring parent. Just as Jesus Christ taught us throughout the few, short years that this world was graced by His presence.

www.ingramcontent.com/pod-product-compliance
Lightning Source LLC
Chambersburg PA
CBHW060357130626
46553CB00003B/1275